WHEN YOU WORK OUTSIDE THE HOME

6 STUDIES ON CREATIVE PARENTING FOR WORKING MOMS

DR. JUDY HAMLIN

VICTOR BOOKS

A DIVISION OF SCRIPTURE PRESS PUBLICATIONS INC.
USA CANADA ENGLAND

Copyediting: Pamela T. Campbell
Cover Design: Scott Rattray
Cover Illustration: Robert Bergin
Interior Illustrations: Al Hering

Recommended Dewey Decimal Classification: 243.833
Suggested Subject Heading: BIBLE STUDY: WOMEN
Library of Congress Catalog Card Number: 93-60384
ISBN: 1-56476-074-X

1   2   3   4   5   6   7   8   9   10 Printing/Year 97   96   95   94   93

VICTOR BOOKS
A division of SP Publications, Inc.
Wheaton, Illinois 60187

CONTENTS

To Penny with love

INTRODUCTION

This study is for mothers who hold jobs or pursue activities outside the home for substantial parts of each weekday. It is a very personal study, influenced by my own experiences, my highs and lows, and my ultimate realization that God's Scripture provides a framework for successful working moms.

It is written to help us deal with the "real" challenges—finding quality time for our children, modeling positive roles for them, finding a partnership and balance with our husbands in child-rearing. It also considers "intangibles," such as guilt, which affects a mother's emotional and mental frame of mind. It even offers a look at the issues from the child's perspective.

While mistakes can be forgiven, I believe we are given experiences to share with others which can turn negatives into positives. Once a young rushed mother, I now look forward with great anticipation to being a better grandparent.

Each session in this study includes:

☐ *Scripture* and *Purpose* statements reflect the goals of the session.

☐ *Looking Inside* combines questions with illustrations to be used as conversation starters.

☐ *Topical Text* prompts participants to work through specific issues.

☐ *Scriptures* that speak to those specific issues.

☐ *Prayer Together* encourages participants to develop the discipline of prayer and praise.

In the *Leader's Notes* you will find background information, additional questions, and an outline for each session. During the course of this study the Holy Spirit might prompt you to make a decision to receive Jesus Christ as your Lord and Savior. If this happens, turn to the back of the study and review the Five Steps. You may do this alone, with a friend, or with your group leader. Record your spiritual birthday, then read, claim, and receive God's gifts.

HUGS

It's wondrous what a hug can do.
A hug can cheer you when you're blue.
A hug can say, "I love you so"
Or, "I hate to see you go."
A hug is "Welcome back again,"
And "Great to see you! Where've you been?"
A hug can soothe a small child's pain
And bring a rainbow after rain.
The hug, there's just no doubt about it—
We scarcely could survive without it!
A hug delights and warms and charms
It must be why God gave us arms.
Hugs are great for fathers and mothers,
Sweet for sisters, swell for brothers;
And chances are your favorite aunts
Love them more than potted plants.
Kittens crave them, puppies love them;
Heads of states are not above them
A hug can break the language barrier,
And make travel so much merrier.
No need to fret about your store of 'em'
The more you give, the more there's more of 'em.
So stretch those arms without delay
And give someone a hug today!

Author unknown

What Your Child Needs

SCRIPTURE

"Behold, children are a gift of the Lord" *(Psalm 127:3, NASB)*.

PURPOSE

To become aware of children's needs as children view them.

LOOKING INSIDE

1. Insert the name(s) of your child(ren) and an appropriate personal characteristic in the following statement:

"I delight in _____ way of _____."
            (child's name)

2. Which of three actions—listening, spending time, or being sensitive—do you think your child would say you do best?

3. Which of your traits or talents—cooking, sewing, art, music, etc.—do you think your child would say is most outstanding?

BECOME A BETTER LISTENER

Before you can meet your children's needs and develop better relationships with them, you must learn to be a better listener. Although any dialogue will be a step in the right direction, the following questions can help you get your children to open up. Use these and other questions to get a good glimpse into your children's minds.

8   WHEN YOU WORK OUTSIDE THE HOME

1. When you wake up in the morning, what's the first thing you like to do?

2. What is the first thing you like to do when you get home in the afternoon?

3. What is your favorite family activity?

4. What do you do just before going to bed?

5. If you could make one change in your activities, what would it be?

6. What is your definition of *mother?*

7. What is your definition of *father?*

8. What do you like most about being a child?

9. Describe a special "event" you have shared with your family. What made it so special?

TAKE FIVE

Take five minutes and respond to the questions from your child's viewpoint—what you *think* your child would say. Then, as a group, discuss the findings.

Child's Name			
1.			
2.			
3.			
4.			
5.			
6.			
7.			
8.			
9.			

Parents should strive to fill three main needs for their children:

1. A sense of _____ .

2. A sense of _____ .

3. Being made to feel "_____."

MOTHERHOOD — A CHILD'S DEFINITION
The following are excerpts of children's definitions of *mother*.

"Mom spends time with me."
"Mom makes things special."
"We take trips together."
"Mom makes me brush my teeth."
"Mom reads to me at night."
"Mom cooks."
"Mom helps out at school."
"Mom takes me and my friends to ball practice."
"Mom understands when I make boo boos."

MOTHERHOOD — A BIBLICAL DEFINITION
The Scriptures often use metaphors of mother and child to describe our relationship to God.

"But we were gentle among you, like a mother caring for her little children" (1 Thessalonians 2:7).

_____

"My heart is not proud, O LORD, my eyes are not haughty; I do not concern myself with great matters or things too wonderful for me. But I have stilled and quieted my soul; like a weaned child with its mother, like a weaned child is my soul within me" (Psalm 131:1-2).

_____

_____

_____

_____

"Can a mother forget the baby at her breast and have no compassion on the child she has borne? Though she may

forget, I will not forget you!" (Isaiah
49:15)

_____

"I would lead you and bring you to my
mother's house — she who has taught
me" (Song of Songs 8:2).

_____

PRAYING TOGETHER

Even though our schedules are busy we can create prayer plans
that will help us become more effective mothers. Concentrate
today on three main areas: asking for wisdom, sensitivity, and
keeping a sense of humor as we deal with our children.

_Father, help me become more aware of my children's specific
needs._

Heavenly Father, help me be more compassionate.

Father, I need help in teaching _____. _Give me
patience and wisdom._

_Father, help me lighten up, laugh, and have fun with my
children._

_Father, be with me this week as I spend time with my child(ren).
As we review the questions, help me identify their needs and
what they consider important._

THIS WEEK

Schedule an informal appointment with each of your children.
Make this time one-on-one, private, and pay personal attention
to each child. That's something every child longs for, and you
will get more individualistic answers. Ask the questions from this
study. Afterward, make notes and bring them to the next session.
Listen carefully for messages that help you identify what a child
feels contributes to "creating a memory," or being made to "feel
special." Both contribute to self-esteem.

THE FIRST 15 MINUTES

SCRIPTURE
"Behold the farmer waits for the precious produce of the soil, being patient about it, until it gets the early and late rains" *(James 5:7c, NASB)*.

PURPOSE
To identify what's important for children to "experience" prior to beginning their day.

LOOKING INSIDE
1. What do you remember most about "mornings" when you were growing up?

2. What "one thing" would you have changed about mornings during your childhood?

3. Did your parents treat you and your siblings impartially? Give an example.

POSSIBLE MORNING ACTIVITIES

The following chart lists things that can occur when the family is starting the day. For each activity, check how often it occurs in your home.

ACTIVITIES	NEVER	SELDOM	SOMETIMES	OFTEN	ALWAYS
Pleasant "wake-up" method					
Morning hug					
Morning kiss					
Breakfast at the table as a family					
Pleasant conversation					
*Daily checklist					
Lunchbox surprise					

*Create a checklist for morning review. The list will include items to be remembered before leaving home for the day (i.e., favorite toy, homework, lunch or lunch money, kiss from mom, etc.).

List the activities you would like to move up to an OFTEN or ALWAYS status.

_____   _____
_____   _____
_____   _____

TAKE FIVE

With your neighbor, brainstorm how you plan to change your routine.

GETTING CLOSER

It is easier to get close to your children when you have creative ideas or give the things you already do funny names. Review this list from "Tips for Getting Closer to Your Child" (*McCall's*, May 1988, p. 43). Then create your own ideas.

■ **Reveille!**
It's a military tradition for troops to awaken to the sound of a bugle. You can establish a similar tradition, using favorite records or cassettes to announce the start of the day.

■ **Reverse Snuggles**
Kids love to crawl into their parents' bed. Why not reverse the process and crawl into bed with your sleepy youngsters for a minute or two when they first open their eyes? Morning cuddling can start everyone's day off right.

■ **Happygrams**
Happygrams are brief personal notes expressing appreciation and affection. Kids delight in finding them under their cereal bowls, in their lunch boxes, or stuck inside their shoes.

ENCOURAGEMENT, NOT CONDEMNATION

Sometimes we don't realize how we are responding to others. Our minds are already on the work schedule of the day, problems to solve, reports to get out, etc. It is important that we understand how we may be coming across to others, especially our children. This will be a step toward change. Use 1 Corinthians 13:4-13 to evaluate yourself on how you respond to your children.

	Usually	Some-times	Rarely
■ patient	_____	_____	_____
■ kind	_____	_____	_____
■ not envious	_____	_____	_____
■ not boastful	_____	_____	_____
■ not proud	_____	_____	_____
■ not rude	_____	_____	_____
■ not self-centered	_____	_____	_____
■ not easily angered	_____	_____	_____
■ not keeping records of wrongs	_____	_____	_____
■ not devious	_____	_____	_____
■ celebrate truth	_____	_____	_____
■ protective of children	_____	_____	_____

	Usually	Some-times	Rarely
■ always trusting	_____	_____	_____
■ always hoping	_____	_____	_____
■ always persevering	_____	_____	_____
■ always loyal	_____	_____	_____
■ emotionally mature	_____	_____	_____
■ possess faith	_____	_____	_____
■ possess hope	_____	_____	_____
■ possess — especially love	_____	_____	_____

Don't let your evaluation get you down. No one could have a perfect "Usually" score. This checklist provides "a picture of what Jesus meant when He admonished us to love. It's not so much hearts and flowers; it's more like blood, sweat, and tears. Not so much take, but a lot of give. Not as much 'I want' as 'What do you want/need?' Not as much 'I need space' as 'I need to draw closer to you' " (Adapted from: *The Employed Wife: Earning a Living, Making a Home,* Concordia, 1986, pp. 176–77).

PRAYING TOGETHER
Choose the prayer that best fits your need today and pray during the group prayer time.

Father, make me aware daily of the importance of the first minutes with my children.

Father, help me make paying attention to my children each morning a priority.

Lord, help me give willingly of myself, expecting nothing in return.

Heavenly Father, be with my children and help them respond to my desire to change.

Father, help me encourage my children through words and deeds.

THIS WEEK
Discover what your children are thinking. Ask them to complete the following statement without disclosing their responses to

you. Tell each one what you think he or she wrote. Then respond to the list of statements yourself and see what your child thinks.

1. I like to _____ as soon as I wake up.

2. I prefer a kiss, a hug, or both when I wake up?

3. My favorite breakfast food is _____.

4. My favorite thing to wear is _____.

5. My favorite color is _____.

6. My favorite part of morning is _____.

7. My least favorite part of morning is _____.

SEARCHING FOR ANSWERS 3

YOUR CHILD IS UNIQUE

SCRIPTURE
"Train a child in the way he should go, [and in keeping with his individual gift or bent], and when he is old he will not turn from it" *(Proverbs 22:6, AMP)*.

PURPOSE
To discover the individual characteristics of each child and how to "train" him or her individually in a family.

LOOKING INSIDE
1. Which of the following set of characteristics best describes your child or children?

1	2	3	4
Popular	Workaholic	Sensitive	Listener
Funny	Stubborn	Detailed	Adaptable
Talkative	Decisive	Depressed	Indecisive
Unpredictable	Confident	Critical	Worrier

2. Which list of terms best describe you?

3. Think about your children and how they behaved this past week. What one behavior, deed, or action of each child do you feel could improve with training?

Child's name   Behavior

_____   _____

_____   _____

_____   _____

_____   _____

CREATIVE CARING

Dr. Lee Salk, clinical professor of psychology and pediatrics at the New York – Cornell Medical Center, writes: "Parents serve as models for their children – not only for coping with the tribulations of everyday life but in the human values that they practice and transmit to their children" (*McCall's,* June 1991, pp. 83–84).

With each child's individuality in mind our attention and actions must vary from child to child. Following are activities that can be used to open up communication.

- **Pretend to Be a TV Critic**

  Few quality interactions occur during TV viewing. Yet there is a way to help children become more intellectually involved and alert as they watch. Ask them questions like: **What happened on the show? Do you think what you saw happens in real life? Would you like the TV characters as friends? Why?**

- **Interview One Another**

  Families can produce an in-house version of a TV magazine show. One person as designated host interviews other family members with such questions as: **What was the funniest thing that happened to you today? Do you wish you could do part of the day over ? What are your plans for tomorrow?**

- **Evening Activities**

  While you prepare dinner, have the kids supply the entertainment. One child can be the musician, serenading the family with a new song. A child with a creative eye can be the table decorator. Each child can have a new assignment every week.

- **Host an Award Night**

  Award dinners are great ways to make children the center of attention when they've done well on a test, won a game, or gotten a good dental checkup. Fill glasses with juice for toasts. Put flowers in front of the honoree's place at the table. Provide a paper crown. Encourage the guest of honor to describe his or her feelings, accomplishments, and aspirations ("Tips for Getting Closer to Your Child" *McCall's*, May 1988, p. 43).

■ **Family Night**

"Pick one night a week and call it Family Night. Have everyone mark it on his or her schedule well in advance and guard
its priority with great care. A great family night plan is to use
the first one for *family goal setting*. Everyone pitches in the
things he or she would like to see the family accomplish. Joe
White in his book, *Looking for Leadership: Parenting in the
Crisis Years* (Cooperation Challenge, 1984, pp. 133–135),
shares the following way to set those goals:

A. Define the basic categories that your family feels are important, i.e., building great friendships, spiritual growth,
   making the home a "fun spot," effective problem solv-
   ing, etc.
B. Divide each category into specific areas.
C. Write down specific methods to accomplish each goal.
D. Devise a measurable plan of evaluation."

Example Category	Specific Area	Method of Goal Accomplishment	Excellent	Good	Poor
1. Family Spiritual Growth	1. Family Devotions	Just before breakfast each day the family will have a 3–7 minute devotion. The leader will alternate each day around the family.	7 days	4 days	3 or less
	2. Family Prayer	Each night at 10 p.m. the family will meet in Suzie's room for conversa-tional prayer.	7 days	4 days	3 or less
	3. Scripture Memory	Morning devotion will close with a verse to memorize and discuss as a family.	3 verses a week	2 verses a week	1 verse a week

TAKE FIVE

In groups of three help one another plan family nights.

Example Category	Specific Area	Method of Goal Accomplishment	Excellent	Good	Poor

ESTABLISH UNBREAKABLE BOUNDARIES

Sarah Banton, a divorced mother of two sons, was quoted as saying: "Setting the consistent limits kids need takes a lot of energy but if you don't do it, it leads to behavior problems" (*Austin American-Statesman*, October 20, 1992, D18).

"The rod of correction imparts wisdom, but a child left to himself disgraces his mother" (Proverbs 29:15).

Based on the above verse, what imparts wisdom to a child?

"And is well known for her good deeds, such as bringing up children, showing hospitality, washing the feet of the saints, helping those in trouble and devoting herself to all kinds of good deeds" (1 Timothy 5:10).

"And, fathers, do not provoke your children to anger; but bring them up in the discipline and instruction of the Lord" (Ephesians 6:4).

Whose responsibility is it to bring up children?

"Even a child is known by his actions, by whether his conduct is pure and right. Ears that hear and eyes that see—the LORD has made them both" (Proverbs 20:11-12).

How can you help children be more aware of their actions? To develop individuality and personality?

What two senses has God given you in order to better understand your children, and become attentive to their needs?

Let me suggest that those who carry daily planners begin recording your children's actions, reactions, and behavioral patterns so that you can gain a better perspective on what training they need.

PARENTAL BOUNDARIES

It is important to realize that parents are responsible for establishing boundaries for children. Don't fall into the "quality time" trap. It takes time to be a good parent—to establish disciplinary styles and boundaries. The following suggestions can help.

Actions result in consequences. In Scripture we find that Esau traded his inheritance for a meal, and Absalom felt he could defy David and speed up kingship. Their interaction with their parents was just as complicated as ours today, and their actions resulted in consequences which in retrospect shook families and nations. Kathleen Cushman, mother of three and frequent writer on educational matters, writes: "Your style of discipline makes a big difference in how your child learns to cooperate. Give your child authoritative, firm guidance within a warm, supportive relationship. Children with very permissive parents do not learn self-control; those whose parents are too authoritarian don't learn to solve problems for themselves" ("Off to a Great Start!" *Parents*, October 1992, p. 126).

Boundaries are reassuring. In Luke 2:41-51 Jesus, age 12, is traveling with His parents to Jerusalem. When His parents left they assumed Jesus was with them, but after a three-day search they found Him in the temple. His parents did not understand Him when He told them He was in His Father's house. However, He returned to Nazareth and continued in subjection to His parents. "And Jesus kept increasing in wisdom and stature and in favor with God and men" (Luke 2:52).

We've known forever that children test their boundaries as Jesus did at 12. However, during the 18 years between ages 12 and 30—when Jesus began His public ministry—we must assume He was in subjection to His parents. This resulted in His continued growth in wisdom and stature. Psychologists and common sense tell us that our children need and desire structured lives . . . to locate and observe those boundaries. Boundaries provide security and freedom from fear and anxiety about circumstances that result from straying outside the lines. Let your children know you share a need for boundaries. It will make it easier for them to accept their own limitations. Make setting boundaries a family exercise, and pick do-able things—structured homework, limited TV viewing, eating meals together, a five-minute devotional.

PRAYING TOGETHER

Choose the prayer that best fits your need today and pray during the group prayer time.

Father, give me guidance in dealing with my children this week. Allow me to see their differences and begin to deal with each accordingly.

Father, thank You for making each of us unique. I pray this week for fun and for caring for each person in my family.

Heavenly Father, help me think of activities or ideas that will help establish traditions in our home.

Father, help me begin to develop unbreakable boundaries. Make me determined when it is in the best interest of our family.

Father, help me grow as a mother, in supporting my children, supervising and giving them individual attention.

THIS WEEK

Select an activity or family brainstorming session from the Creative Caring section. Record notes for discussion in next week's session.

Note: Child-rearing experts acknowledge the current cultural breakdown—declining values, loss of the family and traditions. To help parents face these and other problems, many experts suggest joining a parent support group. Another suggestion is to develop family traditions (see the Appendix).

The Last 15 Minutes

SCRIPTURE

"Do you not know that in a race all the runners run, but only one gets the prize? Run in such a way as to get the prize" *(1 Corinthians 9:24)*.

PURPOSE

To stress the importance of time with a child prior to the end of the day.

LOOKING INSIDE

1. Of your many accomplishments as a parent to date—helping your child overcome fears, enjoy reading, set priorities, understand money—which do you consider your greatest?

2. As a child what person was there to encourage you with your tough decisions?

3. How do you define *hope?*

BEDTIME EVOLUTION

Have bedtime events changed around your house? Recall the stages of infancy, three years old, and six-plus years old. Circle the changing attitudes, events, or actions that you identify with.

INFANCY	THREE YEARS OLD	SIX-PLUS YEARS OLD
Baby talk	Back talk	Begging
Cuddle to sleep	Sighs of relief	Bribe to go
Bathe in a warm setting, with full attention of parent	Pull kicking and screaming	Bribe to go
Sing songs	Read a short book over and over because the child realizes he or she does not have your full attention.	Bribe to go ("If you go straight to bed, I'll read you two stories tomorrow"). But do we? Threaten ("If you don't go straight to bed, no TV tomorrow night"). What happens?

Bedtime routines can provide happy closures to hassled days. Both you and your children have had to deal with the outside world. Regardless of how tired we are, we need to devote individual attention as we prepare our children for bedtime. Here are some suggestions on how to do this:

■ Focus on good things that occurred during the day.
■ Listen to a child's prayer.
■ Read a book.
■ Sing a song.
■ Give a big hug, kiss, and words of warmth and reassurance — "I Love You."

■ Hold firm to the bedtime hour (there can be exceptions).
■ Don't engage in activities that excite a child before bedtime.

TAKE FIVE

Describe to your neighbor how you spend a typical night at home. Talk about things you would like to change.

THE LAST 15 MINUTES

The Lord's Supper exemplifies what Jesus considered important as He prepared to leave those around Him. His example can serve as a guide for our leaving our children for the night. Knowing that He was not going to be with His disciples much longer, Jesus accomplished several things over this last meal. First, He showed them attention by washing their feet and breaking bread. Second, He exhibited unconditional love toward Judas (even though He knew Judas would deceive Him). Finally, following the meal, Jesus went to the Garden of Gethsemane and prayed for Himself and His followers.

Be aware that your children want and need your attention, unconditional love, and prayer. Reassuring a child at the closing of the day will help him or her develop a feeling of security.

Transition Time

The last 15 minutes of the day can be the most meaningful time with your child because it is the real transitional link between the day you're just finishing and tomorrow. It's especially important to children, since they haven't yet developed senses of time and relativity.

The problem is, the last 15 minutes are usually the toughest for working moms—for concentration and meaningful relationships. So what do you have to do to make it work? You can find the answer in Matthew 6:25.

"Therefore I tell you, do not worry about your life, what you will eat or drink; or about your body, what you will wear. Is not life more important than food, and the body more important than clothes?" (Matthew 6:25)

Don't be anxious; plan ahead.

Recap Time

Once you've completed your activities, recap the day from the child's perspective and involve him or her in recalling major activities, details, whatever comes up. Give your child a synopsis of *your* day; this gives a sense of adult interaction and your commitment to this precious time.

The New Testament contains many letters written by the disciples to recount the event of their lives. The letters were written to Christian brothers and sisters. It would be good for you to record the daily events of your children, to document memories and create a history of what's important to them. The Apostle Paul wrote: "But that you also may know about my circumstances, how I am doing" (Ephesians 6:21a, NASB). Create a journal.

Tucking-in Prayer

Before tucking in, be sure to pray in short, simple sentences. Let your child talk about what's important to him or her and share what's important to you. Sharing is a great habit to develop, and it will make prayer much easier through practice and your model.

Follow-up Prayer

Once your child is asleep, follow up with a prayer time of your own. This will become a good transition from the quality time spent with your child to beginning some quality time of your own.

In 2 Timothy 1:5, Paul remembers faithful women who proceeded the faith of others. Go before your children, offering prayer on their behalf. In his book, *The Man in the Mirror* (Wolgemuth & Hyatt, 1989), Patrick M. Morley provides a list of subjects he uses to pray for his children. He invites us all to adapt the list, issuing this challenge: "No man [woman] would be unwilling to die for his [her] children. How much more important to live for them" (p. 97). His list of subjects includes (p. 97):

A saving faith (thanksgiving if already Christian)
A growing faith
An independent faith (as they grow up)
To be strong and healthy in mind, body, and spirit

A sense of destiny (purpose)
A call to excellence
To understand the ministry God has for them
To acquire wisdom
Protection from drugs, alcohol, and premarital sex
The mate God has for them (alive somewhere, needing prayer)
Glorify the Lord in everything

PRAYING TOGETHER

Choose the prayer that best fits your need today and pray during the group prayer time.

Thank You, Father, for the great times and memories you've given me and my daughter/son _____.

Father, thank You for the special time each night you give me with _____.

Dear Lord, help me give _____ the love and encouragement he/she needs day by day.

Father, give me the right words as I seek to help my friend _____ relate with her children.

THIS WEEK

The following resources are excellent for mothers—especially those who work. Be able to describe one example next week.

Good For Me! poster; *School Days Keepsake Album* (Toys to Grow On, P.O. Box 17, Long Beach, CA 90801).

Marvelous Me: A Learning Works Skills Builder (The Learning Works, 1979).

Bonnie Sose, *Designed by God: So I Must Be Special*; *A New Child Organizer* (Character Builders for Kids).

A Mother's Regrets

SCRIPTURE

"No temptation has seized you except what is common to man. And God is faithful; He will not let you be tempted beyond what you can bear. But when you are tempted, He will also provide a way out so that you can stand up under it" (1 Corinthians 10:13).

PURPOSE

To put guilt and forgiveness in proper perspective, allowing inner peace which makes effective parenting possible.

LOOKING INSIDE

1. What do you feel is the best thing you've done for each of your children?

2. What do you feel is the most important thing you've failed to do for each of your children?

HERE'S GOOD NEWS FOR WORKING MOMS!

Some say that being a parent, wife, and worker triples a woman's burden. New research says it triples her joy. "The more roles a woman has, the more opportunity she has to obtain satisfaction, success, and rewards," says researcher Toni Antonucci, Ph.D., professor of psychology at the University of Michigan in Ann Arbor, who measured the quality of life, frequency of depression, and self-esteem of 2,500 women.

Her study found that despite the everyday strains and stresses of raising a family, mothers are physically healthier and have higher self-esteem than single or married women without children. Although her study focused on working moms, Antonucci believes that any outside activity — whether it be a volunteer job, a hobby, or even regular exercise — can lead to healthier emotional life.

In fact, Antonucci reports that multiple roles may even alleviate stress. "For instance, if your job is unrewarding but your kids are blossoming, the situation at work doesn't seem so devastating," says Antonucci.

Mothers are also physically healthier because they tend to take good care of themselves. "They are the people who buckle their seat belts, don't smoke, don't drink, eat regularly, and don't snack as much, probably because they know that there are others — namely their husband and kids — who depend on them," observes Antonucci (*Parents Magazine*, October 1992, p. 17).

HOW CONFIDENT ARE YOU?

Some common, thoroughly modern assumptions about how to correctly rear children can actually sabotage parental authority and leave us feeling smaller than our children. Do you agree or disagree with the following statements? Pay close attention to your instinctive response.

	Agree	Disagree
1. The mistakes we made before our child was five are irreversible.	——	——
2. When you get right down to it, mothers are primarily to blame for children's problems.	——	——
3. I'm trying to raise my kids exactly the opposite from the way I was raised.	——	——
4. After I lay down the law, I'm afraid to change my mind for fear of being inconsistent.	——	——
5. If I don't listen to my child when she wants to talk, she'll never open up again.	——	——
6. I've got to make every free moment my child and I spend together count.	——	——
7. I should never burden my kid with my unparentlike emotions, such as hurt, need, and self-doubt.	——	——
8. Peer groups are for kids. I'm hesitant to network with other parents for support because my kid doesn't think it's right for parents to talk to each other.	——	——
9. I live in dread of adolescence.	——	——
10. I'd better stick to expert opinions, not my own instincts.	——	——

Adapted from "How Confident Are You?" *McCall's*, November 1991, p. 48.

Remember, there's no shame in admitting that we've been imperfect mothers. Our goal is improvement, even if it has to wait for grandchildren to benefit. Reread and see if you agree with your first answers.

WOMEN IN THE 90s

Like it or not, children listen to what high profile people say. They're just as prone (as we were!) to discount what mom or dad have to say, in favor of the opinions of their peers, TV or movie stars, and the like. Don't ignore or fight this; introduce ideas from high profile people whom you respect or whose opinions you respect. That way, you can reinforce your own values, while showing children it's OK to consider independent viewpoints.

Discuss each of the following excerpts ("Passion, A Pulitzer and a Day in Her PJs," *McCall's*, November 1991, pp. 130–135) and what insights they provide for mothering in the 90s.

Florence (Flo-Jo) Griffith-Joyner

Occupation: Former Olympic gold medalist; now clothing designer; children's book author; actress
Family: Married; one child
Greatest Influence: "The main reason I wanted to be successful was to get out of the [Watts] ghetto. I was fortunate in that I had a mother who encouraged me to be different and a father who taught me discipline."
Greatest motivator: "Whenever I doubted my capabilities, I read the Scriptures. That, and my faith in God, helped me to overcome my fears."

Chris Evert-Mills

Occupation: Ex-tennis pro; sports broadcaster; president of the Women's Tennis Association
Family: Divorced and remarried; one child
Her Marriage: "You have to have that passion for him as a person—not only in a physical way, but also the kind that when he walks through the door you're just so happy to see him."
Greatest fear: "Childbirth. And the enormous responsibility of being totally unselfish and giving to another human being scares me sometimes."

Marian Wright Edelman

Occupation: Founder and president of the Children's Defense Fund, a national advocacy organization for children's issues
Family: Married; three children
Greatest influence: "What I do today is an extension of what

caring adults in my childhood did with me. My parents [a Baptist minister and a church organist] were extraordinary role models who were able to mix parenting with community involvement. And the fact that I am a woman, a black woman, who grew up in a segregated southern town has a lot to do with [my activism]."

Issue for the 90s: "We have to confront what I view as the great gap and hypocrisy between what we say we believe about kids and what we do. I see the 1990s as being a time when children and families will be central to the domestic policy debate, because otherwise I don't think America is going to have a future that's worth having."

Jeanne White

Occupation: AIDS activist

Family: Single mother; one daughter (son Ryan, 18, died of AIDS last year)

Attitude toward work: "Now I look at what I'm doing as just a job. I don't bring it home at the end of the day."

CHILDREN WEATHERING THE STORM

Just as Jesus admonished us to live in the present . . .

> "Therefore do not worry about tomorrow, for tomorrow will worry about itself. Each day has enough trouble of its own" (Matthew 6:34). . .

we must parent in the present as well. We can learn from mistakes and plan for the future—short term and long term. Our children will have plenty of needs, questions, and problems to deal with today. This day will be just as vital in their development as any in their lives.

Some specific things we need to give our children daily can be found in the story of Samuel. Hannah, Samuel's mother, had been barren for years. Distraught, she bargained with the Lord that if He would give her a son, she would give him back to the Lord. Once weaned, she gave Samuel to Eli the priest to begin his lifetime service. From his mother, Samuel received *destiny*—from birth he was marked for God. Samuel, by obeying, became who God intended him to be.

From his father, Samuel received *humility,* which he demonstrated through his obedience, prayer, and sacrifices to God.

From both parents he received *honesty,* a willingness to admit when he was right or wrong.

Samuel also learned *flexibility.* Although given to God, he met God as a youth, knew Him as a friend, and trusted Him. That destiny, humility, honesty, and flexibility provided Samuel with a stable life.

REVIEW

We learn from Scripture and life experiences that it's never too late to improve mother/child relationships. Many teen and young adult difficulties stem from childhood problems or situations or relationships left unaddressed.

If there's one truth we must acknowledge and act on, it is that we can change and improve. What we do from now on can make a positive difference. We cannot wallow in guilt and self-pity over things we have or haven't done or said. We *can* make choices that will benefit us and our children. And we can begin now.

"Do you not know that in a race all the runners run, but only one gets the prize? Run in such a way as to get the prize" (1 Corinthians 9:24).

"Do not be anxious about anything, but in everything, by prayer and petition, with thanksgiving, present your requests to God" (Philippians 4:6).

PRAYING TOGETHER

Choose the prayer that best fits your need today and pray during the group prayer time.

Father, thank You for the gift of my children; and give me Your mind as I make decisions.

Heavenly Father, fill my mind with ideas that will encourage my children.

Father, help me stay fit for the race I have to run. Give me solid feet and Your Word as encouragement to take risks.

Lord, thank You for my job; and help me keep it in perspective, putting my family first.

Father, I look forward to tomorrow and what we can accomplish together for my children.

THIS WEEK

Chart a day's events as carefully and completely as you can. Try to focus on your interaction with your child, or what you learn about his or her interaction with others — friends, teacher, grandparents, neighbors. Be honest. Write down positive, negative, and neutral occurrences. Bring your notes to the next session.

SEARCHING FOR ANSWERS 6

SHARED APRONSTRINGS

SCRIPTURE

"Jesus gave them this answer: 'I tell you the truth, the Son can do nothing by Himself; He can do only what He sees His Father doing, because whatever the Father does the Son also does' " (John 5:19).

PURPOSE

To recognize, understand, and encourage the role of the father (male) to a son or daughter.

LOOKING INSIDE

1. How much time does your spouse spend with each child?

2. What do you feel would be each child's response to the question, "Do you know your father loves you?"

GOOD NEWS FOR WORKING MOMS

Through extensive research Rosalind C. Barnett, psychologist and senior research associate at the Wellesley College Center for Research on Women, and Caryl Rivers, professor of journalism at Boston University and author of *More Joy Than Rage*, have found the following good news for working mothers.

- Children in two-income families don't see as much stereotyped gender roles since fathers handle more child care.

- The main problems for working mothers are poor child care and family relations. (See Appendix B.)

■ In two-income families, children don't suffer form neglect — both parents focus on the kids on weekends. Couples tend to suffer instead.

■ Women can work and not bring problems home, but men have difficulty taking on chores.

■ Married women with great jobs have high mental wellness. Career women suffer the least from stress.

■ Men are recognizing their vital role in the success of the family unit.

From *Working Women,* "The Myth of the Miserable Working Woman" (February 1992), pp. 62, 64–65, 83.

List some benefits and areas for improvement for working moms.

Benefits   Areas for improvement
_____   _____
_____   _____
_____   _____
_____   _____
_____   _____
_____   _____

TIMES ARE CHANGING

Nothing is more constant than change. And nowhere is change more apparent than in interfamily relationships. Joseph Coleman ("Diaper Law May Change Men's Room," *Austin American-Statesman,* July 13, 1992, A6) reports that fathers find it difficult to change diapers in public places because of no changing tables, so legislatures are passing bills to rectify the problem. As men are becoming more involved with young children, it has become a necessity. More men are taking babies on car and airplane trips and to ballgames.

In *American Demographics* (August 1990), Bickley Townsend, vice president of The Roper Organization, and Kathleen O'Neil, a Roper public opinion analyst, report survey findings concerning changing roles of women:

In many respects, the two sexes agree. Men express strong and consistent support for women's improved status in society. They, like women, believe that sex discrimination remains an important problem in the workplace. And they agree that the most tangible way in which they could help women balance jobs and family is to take on more household work.

But men are also a major cause of resentment and stress for American women. In 1970, most women were concerned about getting men to share household chores. Now, a generation of sweeping change later, women's expectations have outpaced the change in men's behavior. Token help with the dishes or the children no longer inspires women's gratitude; instead, as women contribute more to the family income, they expect in return a more equal division of the household responsibilities.

Next to money, "How much my mate helps around the house" is the single biggest cause of resentment among women who are married or living as if married, with 52% citing this as a problem. Improvement in this area is one of the top things women cite when they consider what would make their lives better (p. 28).

"What could change to help women balance their triple role of worker, mother, wife? Far and away the answer, cited by seven in ten women, is more help from men with household and child care responsibilities. And almost as many men as women—64 percent—agree that by doing more at home, men could help women balance work and family" (p. 32).

The outlook for the future, "women's home life will become easier. Men's performance at home has failed to measure up to women's expectations. But the outlook is positive, because men know they need to become more involved in household responsibilities. Look for beliefs to be transformed into behavior" (p. 32).

Based on your experience, what are some changes occurring in men/women relationships and roles?

1. _____

2. _____

3. _____

4. _____

5. _____

DIVORCED PARENTS

With the huge number of divorced couples with children (in 1990, there were 1,175,000 divorced couples and 1,045,750 children), it's vital that fathers and mothers cooperate when it comes to their children's best interests. A routine of custody and activities provides structure and stability for children.

A woman who asks for financial, emotional, or child-rearing help from an ex-husband isn't indicating failure; she's executing good judgment. Cooperation between divorced/separated parents produces better adjusted children and relief for the spouse with primary custody.

Divorced parents need to agree on things such as discipline, bedtime, help with schoolwork, and extracurricular activities. Then children will feel as if they have *two* parents and get consistent guidance.

COMMUNICATION

The most useful tool in a positive relationship is good communication. Conversely, one of the main culprits in a dysfunctional situation is poor communication.

1. Men and women communicate differently. If a woman were to say, "The house is really messy but I don't have time to clean up," she expects him to offer to clean up while she's grocery shopping. A more direct request is more likely to get the desired result (Deborah Tannen, "How to Close the Communication Gap Between Men and Women," *McCall's,* May 1991, p. 100).

2. Poor communication can wreck any situation. Often we must experience a negative situation for a long time before "the lightbulb comes on." Harris Brandt wrote a wonderful article ("Mom for a Month: How Difficult Can Running the Household Be?" *Parents* Magazine, October 1992, pp. 77–70) on how a father responded to learning that his pregnant wife had to spend the last month in bed. First, he had to deal with the incredible schedule that she had kept, unknown to him: kids to school at different times; carpools; kids out of school and to afternoon events at different times and places. Add a wife needing food, drink, and care; then entertaining and refereeing the kids.

It wasn't surprising that the result was self-pity, resentment, and a sense of infringement on his rights. Finally, the man "got it." He learned that he can make things *easier*, not more difficult. By understanding that his wife is the one physically ailing, not him, his whole attitude changes. Remarkably, the situation then changes for the better. His lightbulb came on!

The mothers of his kids' friends volunteer to help with carpooling and baby-sitting. The in-laws cook and run errands. A new, positive routine sets in. And sure enough, when the baby comes and things return to normal, he actually *misses* his role.

Through adversity we can learn to comunicate and become more effective. Remember, we live our lives between our ears. Make it a happy space. Only by examining our circumstances, facing self-pity, doubt, and anxiety, can we learn to fully enjoy our circumstances.

PARENTING TIPS
In their book, *Quality Parenting* (Random House, Inc., 1987), Linda Alvert and Michael Popkin share the following tips for parenting skills that we sometimes overlook:

Making Kids Feel Grown Up
My father asks me what I think of something that's happening on his job. I like to give my opinion, and it feels great that what I think means something to him.

Kids always love to pretend they're grown up. But we can also offer them real opportunities to think and act in an adult manner by asking for their opinions and preferences on matters that relate to their own care. We can also let them participate in making plans that affect the whole family. This in turn often helps children act more responsibly.

Not Being Too Serious
We were on a family camping trip. It started to rain, and everyone was disappointed. Dad started singing a chorus of "Singing in the Rain," and pretty soon we were singing all the rain songs we knew. It turned out to be one of our best trips.

It seems that for many kids having their parents in a good mood is the exception, not the rule. We can develop a more easygoing attitude by refusing to take things too seriously and not overreacting to a child's every transgression.

Making It Fun
Once a week, in October, we all have to go out and rake leaves. After a while it gets boring. Then Dad stops and throws us in a big pile of leaves. It's fun.

Fun is the universal language, and children speak it instinctively. Make things fun by doing the unexpected, providing a twist to the usual routine. Get in touch with the childlike part of your personality and do things with your children that generally only kids do.

TAKE FIVE
In groups of three, create your own ideas for one of the three areas described above.

_____

_____

_____

BIBLICAL GUIDANCE FOR FATHERS
The Bible offers specific guidance for fathers who want to build good family relationships by modeling.

A university dean once visited the family of two of his students on a holiday. The son and daughter spoke so highly of their successful father that the dean couldn't wait to meet him.

When he arrived, he found that the father's "success" had nothing to do with prosperity. The man cheerfully helped his wife with household chores; washed his son's car; drove a truck so his daughter could use his car; slept on a cot so the dean would be treated royally and the kids could have their own bedrooms. The attitude was contagious. Soon the dean was pitching in with the entire family, and it became a memorable weekend.

That father had set the "tone" for good family relationships.

It's *always* more effective for fathers to lead by example and through love and concern. That leadership results in better current situations and better-prepared futures for everyone in the family.

Read and discuss the following Scriptures as they relate to a father's modeling. Identify which part of the previous story is a practical example of the Scripture.

"Then make my joy complete by being like-minded, having the same love, being one in spirit and purpose. Do nothing out of selfish ambition or vain conceit, but in humility consider others better than yourselves" (Philippians 2:2-3).

"For even the Son of Man did not come to be served, but to serve, and to give His life as a ransom for many" (Mark 10:45).

"Whoever wants to become great among you must be your servant" (Mark 10:43).

"Give, and it will be given to you. A good measure, pressed down, shaken together and running over, will be poured into your lap. For with the measure you use, it will be measured to you" (Luke 6:38).

REFLECTIONS

As you reflect on this lesson, read the following words of Joan Rae Mills.

A Father's Footsteps

Walking with you
I couldn't have considered
asking you to shorten your stride
for in wanting to be like you
yard-long paces
were a pleasurable goal.
Older onlookers smiled,
forgetting perhaps, their own
efforts
to reach a hero's ground.

Those footsteps were soon
matched
for challenges driven
by childish admiration
are often attained.

Now, I walk without you.
Remembering that your steps
challenged me,
I lengthen my stride;
knowing you led me right,
I plan my direction;
knowing now that little feet
follow me
I can walk confidently . . .
following a father's footsteps
that mark a firm, clear trail.

(*Virtue*, May/June 1988, p. 39)

Be determined to encourage family interactions and conduct family planning sessions. For your husband, create situations made to succeed. Make father-child time easy with activity suggestions. Help with arrangements and be available for taking care of your other children so dad can spend one-on-one time with each child.

PRAYING TOGETHER

Turn to one of the previous sessions and select a prayer or take this opportunity to write your own prayer. My prayer:

_____

_____

_____

_____

THIS WEEK

As we close this study, your assignment is to continue to "run the race" of worker, wife, and mom with God's help.

LEADER'S NOTES 1
WHAT YOUR CHILD NEEDS

WELCOME

Welcome each mom to the group. Point out that this book includes Scripture, but they may wish to bring their own Bibles. Prayer will be sentence prayers with samples provided. Participation is optional—whenever they feel comfortable, they may pray aloud.

PURPOSE

Have a volunteer read aloud the Scripture and Purpose statement. Stress the importance of listening to our children in order to become aware of their needs.

LOOKING INSIDE

Ask volunteers to respond to the questions, giving everyone an opportunity to speak. In a new group it may be necessary for you to go first.

For Question #1 give the following example: I delight in Andy's way of being determined.

On Question #2, comment that three phrases can add greatly to the harmony of one's family—"please," "thank you," and "I'm sorry." Each phrase reflects caring, respect, and sensitivity to children. When we use these phrases, we model behavior that will enrich our children's lives and relationships with others.

BECOME A BETTER LISTENER

Read the questions aloud and discuss how they can help children to open up. Then, ask group members to circle those questions that include something to be done with a child. Discuss the importance of being conscious of children's needs to the point where we may have to sacrifice some of our own. Allow time if several would like to share.

TAKE FIVE

Have each participant respond to the questions from their children's viewpoints—what they *think* their children would say.

Take time to randomly read the questions and have one or two respond to each.

Discuss the three main needs that children have.

1. A sense of *belonging.* Linda Albert and Michael Popkin, family therapists who specialize in parent education, write in their book *Quality Parenting* (Random House, 1987) that "doing things as a family—attending religious services, sharing vacations, going out to dinner—contributes to a strong sense of belonging and provides kids with a feeling of security that can last a lifetime."

2. A sense of *security.* Charles R. Swindoll in *You and Your Child* (Bantam, 1984) states: "The single most important ingredient contributing to knowing your child is 'sensitivity.' A parent who is genuinely sensitive to their child will generally have little difficulty coming to know their child."

3. Being made to feel *"special."* Albert and Popkin tell us that "to a young child, the world can seem like a huge and dangerous place over which he has no control. The time a parent spends caring for her child makes him/her feel safe, secure, and special. We show caring when we are empathetic to our youngsters' problems or when we offer help to a child overwhelmed with school work or chores."

MOTHERHOOD—A CHILD'S DEFINITION
Take a few minutes to review the comments, asking the group what their children might add.

MOTHERHOOD—A BIBLICAL DEFINITION
Have volunteers read each Scripture aloud. Instruct group members to highlight the key words found in each passage. List the characteristics of motherhood in each passage. Some are obvious, others are implied. Don't look for one right answer—allow group members to share what they see in the passage. Use the following responses as prompters if needed.

1 Thessalonians 2:7   gentle style
Psalm 131:1-2   rest

	contented
	protection
	security
Isaiah 49:15	compassion
Song of Songs 8:2	teaches

As a group, using the responses from the Scripture, write a definition of *mother.*

PRAYING TOGETHER

Take about five minutes for prayer. This will vary depending on the size of your group. Since praying in a group may be new for many, use the printed prayers, allowing each person to choose one. Then, let volunteers read their prayers. Close the prayer time together.

THIS WEEK

Review the assignment for the week. Tell group members they will want to have separate question sheets for each child, to record responses and add comments following the informal appointments.

LEADER'S NOTES 2
THE FIRST 15 MINUTES

BRIDGE

Ask each group member to describe her appointments with her children. After everyone has had an opportunity to contribute, create two lists: things that create memories for children and things that make children feel special. If you have wall space, post the lists for the remainder of the session.

PURPOSE

Have a volunteer read the Scripture and Purpose statement. Share that a survey on men leaving home in the mornings found that those receiving a big kiss and pleasant greeting from their spouse performed much better at work than those who didn't. Discuss the implications of this study for our children.

LOOKING INSIDE

Have volunteers respond to the questions. Regarding Question #3, ask: **How have your parents' treatment of you affected your own homes and children?**

POSSIBLE MORNING ACTIVITIES

Give the group several minutes to fill in the scale of responses to daily activities. Then have them list the activities they would like to move up to OFTEN or ALWAYS. Ask if anyone is currently using a "daily checklist." Explain that this is one way to eliminate nagging and help get your child organized.

TAKE FIVE

Allow time for groups of two to three to brainstorm ideas for changing their routines.

GETTING CLOSER

It is easier to get close to your children when you have creative ideas or give the things you already do funny names. Review the ideas listed; then, as a group, create three original ideas. You may wish to make appropriate magazines available for group use.

ENCOURAGEMENT, NOT CONDEMNATION

Have a volunteer read 1 Corinthians 13:4-13. Then allow time for each person to evaluate herself. Comment that we are all on a journey and none of us are perfect. What's important is that we seek to improve. To open discussion, share a personal weak area and a strong one, and why you think so.

PRAYING TOGETHER

Spend a minute in silent prayer asking the Holy Spirit to work in the lives of all present. Then allow members to voice printed or spontaneous prayers. Encourage prayer, reminding group members that God does not hear us because of our eloquence or wordiness, but because our hearts and minds are focused on Him, and He cares for us.

THIS WEEK

What fun! Write the questions on pieces of paper for your children. Ask them to respond, then you guess the responses. Then on another sheet, you respond and let them guess. Bring a story from this experience for next week.

LEADER'S NOTES 3
YOUR CHILD IS UNIQUE

BRIDGE

Ask: **How were your mornings this past week?** Have volunteers share the experience of discovering what their children think, and whether they were surprised with the responses. Ask: **What happened when your child guessed your responses? How well did he or she know you?**

PURPOSE

Have a volunteer read the Scripture and Purpose statement. Take this opportunity to stress biblical models of how different children can be. One dramatic example of how different children with similar environments can be occurs in Genesis 25:19-34 and 27:1-35. Jacob and Esau were twin brothers, lived in the same home, were reared in the same environment, but were opposites in nature. Jacob was a deceptive liar, but peaceful, a cook, and more of a domestic person. Esau was a hunter who displayed manly, outdoors characteristics.

LOOKING INSIDE

Questions #1 and #2 deal with the four personality styles as described by Florence Littauer in *Your Personality Tree* (Word, 1986). Column #1 describes the Sanguine; Column #2, Choleric; Column #3, Melancholy; and Column #4, Phlegmatic. While this is a brief introduction I highly recommend a study of the video series *Your Personality Tree* (Word, 1988). I have seen how her study can benefit parents who wonder why their children act as they do. For example, if you are a Choleric personality and have Sanguine, Melancholy, or Choleric personalities under your roof, you need to know about the strengths and weaknesses of each in order to effectively interact with them.

CREATIVE CARING

After introducing this section, have volunteers read each of the activities. Spend time making sure members are clear about how to plan a "family night." Prepare your own example of a family night, share that with the group; then allow members to create their own plans. When you reconvene, ask volunteers to share what they created.

ESTABLISH UNBREAKABLE BOUNDARIES

After introducing this section have volunteers read the Scriptures, posing each question to the group for responses. Make sure you differentiate between parental discipline and child abuse. Stress guidance and discipline; play down physical actions. Review the suggestion for recording in a daily planner. Make the point that childrearing is important and fulfilling; also point out that cooperation between parents is most effective.

PARENTAL BOUNDARIES

Review the three statements and notes dealing with parental boundaries. Have volunteers read each, stopping for comments and questions.

PRAYING TOGETHER

Take time for prayer, remembering to assure participants they don't have to pray. Have participants look at the printed prayer, select one, then begin your prayer time.

THIS WEEK

Review the assignment, encouraging each group member to build in fun.

LEADER'S NOTES 4
THE LAST 15 MINUTES

BRIDGE
Have members describe the experience of implementing a family activity or brainstorming session.

PURPOSE
Have a volunteer read the Scripture and Purpose statement aloud. Review 1 Corinthians 9:24. Does it say:

- If you "run in such a way," you will *always* win?
- If you "run in such a way," you *may* win?
- If you "run in such a way," you will be pleased in doing your best even if you *don't* win?

Since our children will referee the "race" (balancing motherhood, career, and outside interests), there will be many winners, because each child will judge from a different perspective, even children in the same home.

LOOKING INSIDE
Have volunteers respond to the questions. You may want to begin by giving an example of each. The questions will provide participants insights into the importance of encouraging children at the close of each day, both regarding things that happened that day and challenges they will face tomorrow.

BEDTIME EVOLUTION
Discuss the chart, and recall humorous memories of putting children to bed. After everyone has had time to contribute, review the notes following the chart.

TAKE FIVE
In groups of two, describe a typical night at home to one another. Encourage group members to talk about things they would like to add or change about their children's bedtime routines.

THE LAST 15 MINUTES
Read the summary of the Lord's Supper. Then discuss the next four sections—Transition Time, Recap Time, Tucking-in Prayer, and Follow-up Prayer.

Transition Time

Remind your group members that, like anything else worthwhile, the transition time will be successful in direct proportion to their planning. Ask them to think about what they will do with their children and what they will talk about. Encourage them to write it down if they find that helpful. The resource list at the end of Session 4 could be a great help in planning the time together.

Recap Time

If any of your group members are currently doing this, ask volunteers to share their experiences in recapping the day with their children.

Tucking-in Prayer

Reinforce the importance of being a good role model for our children.

Follow-up Prayer

Help your group members realize the importance of their own prayer time, whether they pray while washing dishes at the sink or while preparing for bed. Share when and where *you* have found time to pray for your children. Refer your group to *You've Got What It Takes* (Victor, 1992), a study for women who feel they've got more than they can handle. Session 5 of that book — "How to Begin the Process of Worship" — tells how to organize for prayer time.

PRAYING TOGETHER

Take time for prayer, remembering to assure participants they don't have to pray. Have participants look at the printed prayers, select one, then begin your prayer time.

THIS WEEK

Review the list of resources, adding others you may have found. Be ready to give locations of bookstores or libraries in your area for group members' research.

LEADER'S NOTES 5
A MOTHER'S REGRETS

BRIDGE
Take time to discuss the additional resources gathered for this session. Focus on the positive, uplifting relationships working moms can have with their children, especially at the day's end.

PURPOSE
Have a volunteer read the Scripture and Purpose statement. Give an example from your experience of God's faithfulness in providing help when you were distraught.

LOOKING INSIDE
In this session you will look at ways to deal with guilt, understand forgiveness, and become a better parent. Have volunteers respond to the two questions, giving everyone a chance to talk.

HERE'S GOOD NEWS FOR WORKING MOMS!
Have volunteers read this section. Take time to discuss the findings, and see if the group agrees that working outside the home can bring benefits to the mother/child relationship.

HOW CONFIDENT ARE YOU?
Give the group several minutes to respond to the statements. The more times you said yes, the less confident you are. Share the following (from *McCall's*, November 1991, p. 48):
- Research over the last 40 years has shown that it's never too late to learn from parenting mistakes.
- "Mothers are to blame" is the biggest myth of modern parenting. In truth, everyone is responsible for the blame and credit—you, your mate, siblings, and the temperament with which your child came into this world.
- Doing everything differently than your parents binds you into rigid child rearing with few creative options.
- Consistency is highly overrated. In fact, kids respond well to thought-out changes of direction. [Remember family brainstorming.]
- You may be too tired or preoccupied to listen all the time. In real life new opportunities keep coming around.

- Ordinary moments together are remembered by kids with as much love as enriched, special times.
- Kids need to see us as real people, not therapists.
- Our children feel better when we support and take care of ourselves.
- Who doesn't anticipate the teen years with fear and trembling? But extensive research has shown that despite rough times, most parent-child relationships improve during adolescence.
- With a little practice, you'll find that your instincts will take you down the right path—if you have the confidence to stick by them.

WOMEN FOR THE 90s

Review the four women and their thoughts. Have group members highlight key points.

1. Encouragement, discipline, overcoming fear with faith and God's Word.
2. Everyone has reservations regarding parenting skills.
3. Parents as role models. Actions may speak louder than words but they must be one and the same. Build up the family.
4. Family comes before work.

CHILDREN WEATHERING THE STORM

In groups of three, have participants read this section. Then have them choose one area (destiny, humility, honesty, or flexibility) and discuss what they provide each day for their children.

REVIEW

Reassemble the group and emphasize that it's never too late to begin building a positive relationship with a child. Encourage members to memorize the two Scriptures in order to provide support to everyday mother/child challenges.

PRAYING TOGETHER

As you close the prayer time, allow a minute for each mother to pray silently and specifically for each of her children by name.

THIS WEEK

Review the assignment.

LEADER'S NOTES 6
SHARED APRONSTRINGS

BRIDGE
Have participants share the notes taken this past week on observations they made regarding their children's interactions with other people.

PURPOSE
Have a volunteer read the opening Scripture and Purpose statement. Comment on the importance of male "role models" for our children.

LOOKING INSIDE
Encourage group members to describe the time their husbands spend with their children and the depth of the relationship.

GOOD NEWS FOR WORKING MOMS
After introducing this section, have volunteers read the research findings. Then, as a group, discuss and record both benefits and areas for improvement.

TIMES ARE CHANGING
Introduce the section by having volunteers read the information. Then, as a group, discuss and list things that are changing. One good example from the text is society's recognition of the father's role in childrearing. Let the group brainstorm other changes they have observed or experienced.

DIVORCED PARENTS
Have a volunteer read the material on divorced parents. If it applies to you or someone in your group, you may extend the discussion. Ask those who are divorced or separated to share one way they have found to work together with their spouses.

COMMUNICATION
Have volunteers read the two scenarios. Discuss this section based on participants' real-life experiences. If you have a pertinent experience, start the discussion. Then invite participants to share situations which were improved through better communi-

cation, or which deteriorated because of poor communication.

PARENTING TIPS

After having participants read the three tips, have groups of three create their own ideas. Then reassemble and share the ideas.

BIBLICAL GUIDANCE FOR FATHERS

Review the biblical guidance for fathers. Have volunteers read and discuss each Scripture as it relates to a father's modeling. Identify that part of the story which serves as a practical example of the Scripture.

Philippians 2:2-3 (drove a truck; slept on a cot)
Mark 10:45 (washed his son's car)
Mark 10:43 (the whole story)
Luke 6:38 (son and daughter spoke highly of their father)

REFLECTIONS

Read the poem as participants listen. Spend time sharing thoughts.

PRAYING TOGETHER

Let this be a special prayer time. Encourage group members to write their prayers.

THIS WEEK

Encourage each "working mom."

APPENDIX
HOW YOU CAN STRENGTHEN YOUR FAMILY TRADITIONS

Studies show, says Paul Pearsall, Ph.D., that families who cele-brate traditions and rituals are happier than those who don't. Valerie Monroe ("How You Can Strengthen Your Family Tradi-tions," *McCall's,* April 1990, p. 81*)* suggests four ways to build this kind of family identity and strength in your life*:*

1. Recognize your family history. Even a young family has a past. Establish a family archive, no matter how casual — a box of pho-tographs kept in a special place, a collection of videotapes of birthday parties, even holiday cards family members have given one another over the years. This gives special significance to your family as a clan. Recognizing what you've done in the past allows you to repeat it if you choose. Take time to look at old photographs together and talk about personal history.

2. Take cues from your children. Children may be quicker than adults to recognize the potential for turning a routine into a tradi-tion. "But we always do it this way!" is a common refrain from young children who need and want to be grounded in the famil-iar. A child can measure his or her own growth against repeated actions or events. Doing something together is an opportunity for a child to bond with his family, and since the bonding feels good he will naturally look for ways to repeat the experience. Finally, family rituals or traditions give a child a sense of safety and control as he masters the predictable.

3. Give your traditions a name. Whether it's Spaghetti and Meat-ball Day to designate a traditional family supper, or Harvey Day, annually commemorating the family acquisition of a large rabbit, naming a specific family action gives it a distinction that sets it apart from the ordinary.

4. Though the spirit of your traditions may be fun, take your commitment to them seriously. "That calls for making time for your shared rituals," says Pearsall. What effect will your commit-ment have on the family? Rituals and traditions promote a sense of "us," says Pearsall, and if there's one predictor of good mental health, it's a feeling of connection.

FIVE STEPS FOR ACCEPTING JESUS CHRIST AS YOUR PERSONAL LORD AND SAVIOR

"For God so loved the world, that He gave His one and only Son, that whoever believes in Him shall not perish but have eternal life" *(John 3:16)*

ACTION	SCRIPTURE	PRAYER	BENEFITS
1. ADMIT your need	Romans 3:23 Romans 6:23	Acknowledge you are a sinner	Eternal life
2. RECOGNIZE the provision	Romans 5:8 Romans 5:19	Acknowledge Christ died on the cross for you	Provides for your needs
3. ACCEPT forgiveness	Acts 3:19 Ephesians 2:8	Say you are sorry for your old ways and receive forgiveness	Eternal forgiveness
4. INVITE Christ into your life	Romans 10:13	Invite Christ into your heart	Continued relationship in prayer with a living God
5. COMMIT your life to Him	1 Peter 1:2 1 Peter 4:19 2 John 1:6 Psalms 37:4-5	Express your willingness to live for Christ, ask for His help to grow in your knowledge and understanding of Him and His will for your life	Obedience and a disciplined life with Christ will carry over to your personal and work life

DATE OF YOUR SPIRITUAL BIRTHDAY _____

GOD'S GIFTS TO YOU	SCRIPTURE	PRAYER	BENEFITS
HOLY SPIRIT	John 14:14-18, 26 Hebrews 13:6 1 Corinthians 12:4 Matthew 7:11 Galatians 5:22	Thank God for the gift of the Spirit	Comforter Helper Giver of Gifts Fruit of the Spirit
HIS PROMISES	2 Peter 1:3-4 2 Corinthians 12:9 Isaiah 40:31 James 1:5-8 1 John 1:7 Psalms 121:7-8 Isaiah 26:3-4	Ask Christ to reveal all things that are good and pure Give thanks for this special day	Security Power Strength Wisdom Fellowship Preservation Peace